THE SMART WORDS AND WICKED WIT OF JANE AUSTEN

Edited by Max Morris

Skyhorse Publishing
A Herman Graf Book

Copyright © Summersdale Publishers Ltd, 2016
Published by arrangement with Summersdale Publishers Ltd.
First Skyhorse Publishing edition 2017

Skyhorse Publishing books may be purchased in bulk at special discounts
for sales promotion, corporate gifts, fund-raising, or educational purposes.
Special editions can also be created to specifications. For details, contact the
Special Sales Department, Skyhorse Publishing, 307 West 36th Street, 11th
Floor, New York, NY 10018 or info@skyhorsepublishing.com.

Skyhorse® and Skyhorse Publishing® are registered trademarks of Skyhorse
Publishing, Inc.®, a Delaware corporation.

Visit our website at www.skyhorsepublishing.com.

10 9 8 7 6 5 4 3 2

Library of Congress Cataloging-in-Publication Data is available on file.

Image credit: iStock

Print ISBN: 978-1-5107-1581-3
Ebook ISBN: 978-1-5107-1584-4

Printed in China

CONTENTS

A SONG AND DANCE

It was a splendid sight, and she began, for the first time that evening, to feel herself at a ball: she longed to dance, but she had not an acquaintance in the room.

OF CATHERINE MORLAND,
NORTHANGER ABBEY

'There is a fine old saying, which everybody here is of course familiar with: "Keep your breath to cool your porridge"; and I shall keep mine to swell my song.'

ELIZABETH BENNET, *PRIDE AND PREJUDICE*

———◆———

'The little Durands were there, I conclude… with their mouths open to catch the music, like unfledged sparrows ready to be fed.'

MRS SMITH, *PERSUASION*

———◆———

'There are some people who cannot bear a party of pleasure.'

MR WILLOUGHBY, *SENSE AND SENSIBILITY*

'My fingers... do not move over this instrument in the masterly manner which I see so many women's do. They have not the same force or rapidity, and do not produce the same expression. But then I have always supposed it to be my own fault – because I will not take the trouble of practising.'

ELIZABETH BENNET, *PRIDE AND PREJUDICE*

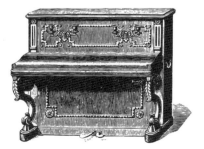

'Do you talk by rule, then,
while you are dancing?'
'Sometimes. One must speak a little,
you know. It would look odd to be
entirely silent for half an hour together;
and yet for the advantage of *some*,
conversation ought to be so arranged
as that they may have the trouble
of saying as little as possible.'

MR DARCY AND ELIZABETH BENNET,
PRIDE AND PREJUDICE

—◆—

'Matrimony and dancing… in both,
man has the advantage of choice,
women only the power of refusal.'

HENRY TILNEY, *NORTHANGER ABBEY*

'People that marry can never part, but must go and keep house together. People that dance only stand opposite each other in a long room for half an hour.'

CATHERINE MORLAND,
NORTHANGER ABBEY

STYLE AND DRESS

'One man's style must not be
the rule of another's.'

MR KNIGHTLEY, *EMMA*

——◆——

He was a stout young man of middling
height, who, with a plain face and
ungraceful form, seemed fearful of
being too handsome unless he wore the
dress of a groom, and too much like a
gentleman unless he were easy where
he ought to be civil, and impudent
where he might be allowed to be easy.

OF JOHN THORPE, *NORTHANGER ABBEY*

You really
must get some flounces.

LETTER TO CASSANDRA

'You are never sure of a good impression being durable.'

CAPTAIN WENTWORTH, *PERSUASION*

———◆———

'A simple style of dress is so infinitely preferable to finery… few people seem to value simplicity of dress – show and finery are everything.'

MRS ELTON, *EMMA*

———◆———

Dress is at all times a frivolous distinction, and excessive solicitude about it often destroys its own aim.

NORTHANGER ABBEY

'Considering how very handsome she is, she appears to be little occupied with it.'

MR KNIGHTLEY ON
EMMA WOODHOUSE, *EMMA*

To be in company, nicely dressed
herself and seeing others nicely
dressed, to sit and smile and look
pretty, and say nothing, was enough
for the happiness of the present hour.

EMMA

———◆———

Dress was her passion. She had a
most harmless delight in being fine.

OF MRS ALLEN, *NORTHANGER ABBEY*

———◆———

'A person may be proud without
being vain. Pride relates more to our
opinion of ourselves; vanity, to what
we would have others think of us.'

MARY BENNET, *PRIDE AND PREJUDICE*

'Nobody can think less of dress in general than I do – but upon such an occasion as this, when every body's eyes are so much upon me, and in compliment to the Westons – who I have no doubt are giving this ball chiefly to do me honour – I would not wish to be inferior to others. And I see very few pearls in the room except mine.'

MRS ELTON, *EMMA*

It would be mortifying to the feelings of many ladies, could they be made to understand how little the heart of man is affected by what is costly or new in their attire; how little it is biased by the texture of their muslin, and how unsusceptible of peculiar tenderness towards the spotted, the sprigged, the mull, or the jackonet.

NORTHANGER ABBEY

———◆———

I cannot help thinking that it is more natural to have flowers grow out of the head than fruit.

LETTER TO CASSANDRA

Woman is fine
for her own
satisfaction alone.

NORTHANGER ABBEY

MEN AND WOMEN

The Miss Dashwoods were young, pretty, and unaffected. It was enough to secure his good opinion; for to be unaffected was all that a pretty girl could want to make her mind as captivating as her person.

SENSE AND SENSIBILITY

'If there is any thing disagreeable going on, men are always sure to get out of it.'

MARY MUSGROVE, *PERSUASION*

———◆———

'Warmth and tenderness of heart, with an affectionate, open manner, will beat all the clearness of head in the world, for attraction, I am sure it will.'

EMMA WOODHOUSE, *EMMA*

———◆———

There certainly are not so many men of large fortune in the world as there are pretty women to deserve them.

MANSFIELD PARK

'Nothing but love,
flirtation, and officers
have been in her head.'

ELIZABETH BENNET ON LYDIA BENNET,
PRIDE AND PREJUDICE

'I am only resolved to act in that manner, which will, in my own opinion, constitute my happiness, without reference to you.'

ELIZABETH BENNET, *PRIDE AND PREJUDICE*

'I think very highly of the understanding of all the women in the world – especially of those – whoever they may be – with whom I happen to be in company.'

HENRY TILNEY, *NORTHANGER ABBEY*

'Man is more robust than woman, but he is not longer lived; which exactly explains my view of the nature of their attachments.'

ANNE ELLIOT, *PERSUASION*

He was exactly formed to engage Marianne's heart.

OF MR WILLOUGHBY,
SENSE AND SENSIBILITY

As for admiration, it was always
very welcome when it came, but
she did not depend on it.

NORTHANGER ABBEY

'He is also handsome… which a young
man ought likewise to be, if he possibly
can. His character is thereby complete.'

ELIZABETH BENNET ON MR BINGLEY,
PRIDE AND PREJUDICE

His air as he walked by the house –
the very sitting of his hat, being all in
proof of how much he was in love!

OF MR ELTON, EMMA

'He must be in love
with you, or he would
never have called us
in this familiar way.'

CHARLOTTE LUCAS ON MR DARCY,
PRIDE AND PREJUDICE

To look almost pretty is an acquisition of higher delight to a girl who has been looking plain for the first fifteen years of her life than a beauty from her cradle can ever receive.

NORTHANGER ABBEY

———◆———

'I have never yet found that the advice of a sister could prevent a young man's being in love if he chose.'

LADY SUSAN VERNON, *LADY SUSAN*

———◆———

'You are conscious that your figures appear to the greatest advantage in walking… I can admire you much better as I sit by the fire.'

MR DARCY, *PRIDE AND PREJUDICE*

'A man does not recover from such a devotion of the heart to such a woman. He ought not; he does not.'

CAPTAIN FREDERICK WENTWORTH,
PERSUASION

'What are young men to
rocks and mountains?'

ELIZABETH BENNET, *PRIDE AND PREJUDICE*

'One man's ways may be as good as
another's, but we all like our own best.'

ADMIRAL CROFT, *PERSUASION*

Handsome is as handsome does.

LETTER TO CASSANDRA

'All the privilege I claim for
my own sex... is that of loving
longest, when existence
or when hope is gone.'

ANNE ELLIOT, *PERSUASION*

'He thoroughly knows his own mind, and acts up to his resolutions: an inestimable quality.'

EDMUND BERTRAM, *MANSFIELD PARK*

———◆———

She attracted him more than he liked... He wisely resolved to be particularly careful that no sign of admiration should *now* escape him.

OF MR DARCY'S ATTEMPTS TO HIDE HIS ATTRACTION TO ELIZABETH BENNET, *PRIDE AND PREJUDICE*

———◆———

It sometimes happens that a woman is handsomer at twenty-nine than she was ten years before.

PERSUASION

'Handsome young men
must have something
to live on as well
as the plain.'

ELIZABETH BENNET,
PRIDE AND PREJUDICE

'In every power, of which taste is the foundation, excellence is pretty fairly divided between the sexes.'

HENRY TILNEY, *NORTHANGER ABBEY*

———◆———

'I will be calm. I will be mistress of myself.'

ELINOR DASHWOOD, *SENSE AND SENSIBILITY*

———◆———

She began to now comprehend that he was exactly the man who, in disposition and talents, would most suit her.

ELIZABETH BENNET, OF MR DARCY, *PRIDE AND PREJUDICE*

Every man is surrounded by a neighbourhood of voluntary spies.

NORTHANGER ABBEY

MATTERS
OF THE
HEART

'At his own ball he offended two or three young ladies, by not asking them to dance; and I spoke to him twice myself, without receiving an answer. Could there be finer symptoms? Is not general incivility the very essence of love?'

ELIZABETH BENNET ON MR BINGLEY'S ATTENTION TO JANE, *PRIDE AND PREJUDICE*

———◆———

'I assure you it was a great compliment if he was [in love with Marianne], for he hardly ever falls in love with any body.'

MRS PALMER ON COLONEL BRANDON, *SENSE AND SENSIBILITY*

'There does seem to be a something in the air of Hartfield which gives love exactly the right direction, and sends it to the very channel where it ought to flow.'

EMMA WOODHOUSE, *EMMA*

'If I could but know his heart,
everything would become easy.'

MARIANNE DASHWOOD,
SENSE AND SENSIBILITY

———◆———

But when a young lady is to be a
heroine, the perverseness of forty
surrounding families cannot prevent
her. Something must and will happen
to throw a hero in her way.

NORTHANGER ABBEY

———◆———

'I suppose there may be a hundred
different ways of being in love.'

EMMA WOODHOUSE, *EMMA*

'It would not be a bad thing for her to be very much in love with a proper object.'

MR KNIGHTLEY ON EMMA WOODHOUSE, *EMMA*

'The mere habit of learning
to love is the thing.'

HENRY TILNEY, *NORTHANGER ABBEY*

———◆———

'The more I know of the world, the more I
am convinced that I shall never see a man
whom I can really love. I require so much!'

MARIANNE DASHWOOD,
SENSE AND SENSIBILITY

———◆———

'I am quite enough in love.'

EMMA WOODHOUSE, *EMMA*

The anxieties of common life began soon to succeed to the alarms of romance.

NORTHANGER ABBEY

She had begun to think he really loved her, and to fancy his affection for her something more than common.

FANNY PRICE'S ASSESSMENT OF MR CRAWFORD, *MANSFIELD PARK*

———◆———

Where youth and diffidence are united, it requires uncommon steadiness of reason to resist the attraction of being called the most charming girl in the world.

NORTHANGER ABBEY

———◆———

'We all know him to be a proud, unpleasant sort of a man; but this would be nothing if you really liked him.'

MR BENNET, *PRIDE AND PREJUDICE*

'I must be in love; I should be the oddest creature in the world if I were not – for a few weeks at least.'

EMMA WOODHOUSE, *EMMA*

'The very first moment I beheld him – my heart was irrecoverably gone.'

ISABELLA THORPE ON JAMES MORLAND, *NORTHANGER ABBEY*

———◆———

'My feelings will not be repressed. You must allow me to tell you how ardently I admire and love you.'

MR DARCY TO ELIZABETH BENNET, *PRIDE AND PREJUDICE*

———◆———

'We all have our best guides within us, if only we would listen.'

FANNY PRICE, *MANSFIELD PARK*

'I could not think about you so much without doting on you, faults and all.'

MR KNIGHTLEY TO EMMA WOODHOUSE, *EMMA*

Darcy had never been so bewitched by any woman as he was by her. He really believed, that were it not for the inferiority of her connections, he should be in some danger.

OF MR DARCY'S FEELINGS TOWARDS ELIZABETH BENNET, *PRIDE AND PREJUDICE*

———◆———

'Very long has it possessed a charm over my fancy; and, if I dared, I would breathe my wishes that the name might never change.'

WILLIAM ELLIOT, *PERSUASION*

'Oh! She is the most
beautiful creature
I ever beheld!'

MR BINGLEY ON JANE BENNET,
PRIDE AND PREJUDICE

'I could not reason so
to a man in love.'

MR KNIGHTLEY, *EMMA*

———◆———

'Next to being married, a girl likes to be
crossed a little in love now and then.'

MR BENNET, *PRIDE AND PREJUDICE*

———◆———

'Sense will always have
attractions for me.'

ELINOR DASHWOOD, *SENSE AND SENSIBILITY*

She had talked her into love;
but, alas! she was not so easily
to be talked out of it.

**EMMA'S THOUGHTS ON HARRIET'S
UNSUITABLE SUITOR, *EMMA***

———◆———

'To be sure, you knew no actual
good of me – but nobody thinks
of *that* when they fall in love.'

**ELIZABETH BENNET TO MR DARCY,
*PRIDE AND PREJUDICE***

'Upon my word, I never saw a young woman so desperately in love in my life!'

MRS JENNINGS ON MARIANNE DASHWOOD, *SENSE AND SENSIBILITY*

'You are too sensible a girl, Lizzy,
to fall in love merely because
you are warned against it.'

MRS GARDINER, *PRIDE AND PREJUDICE*

———◆———

'I feel no sentiment of
approbation inferior to love.'

MRS DASHWOOD, *SENSE AND SENSIBILITY*

'Risk anything rather than her displeasure.'

MR BENNET, *PRIDE AND PREJUDICE*

'In nine cases out of ten, a woman had better show more affection than she feels.'

CHARLOTTE LUCAS, *PRIDE AND PREJUDICE*

———◆———

The enthusiasm of a woman's love is even beyond the biographer's.

MANSFIELD PARK

———◆———

He expressed himself on the occasion as sensibly and as warmly as a man violently in love can be supposed to do.

PRIDE AND PREJUDICE

A young woman in
love always looks –
'like Patience on
a monument
Smiling at Grief.'

NORTHANGER ABBEY

Her heart did whisper that
he had done it for her.

OF ELIZABETH BENNET'S FEELINGS TOWARDS MR
DARCY, *PRIDE AND PREJUDICE*

———◆———

[She] was one of those, who, having
once begun, would be always in love.

OF HARRIET SMITH, *EMMA*

ARTS AND
GRACES

'That is what I like; that is what a young man ought to be. Whatever his pursuits, his eagerness in them should know no moderation, and leave him no sense of fatigue.'

MARIANNE DASHWOOD,
SENSE AND SENSIBILITY

Mrs Goddard was the mistress of a School... a real, honest, old-fashioned Boarding-school, where a reasonable quantity of accomplishments were sold at a reasonable price, and where girls might be sent to be out of the way, and scramble themselves into a little education, without any danger of coming back prodigies.

EMMA

———◆———

'A woman must have a thorough knowledge of music, singing, drawing, dancing, and the modern languages, to deserve the word; and besides all this, she must possess a certain something in her air and manner of walking, the tone of her voice, her address and expressions, or the word will be but half-deserved.'

CAROLINE BINGLEY ON BEING ACCOMPLISHED, *PRIDE AND PREJUDICE*

She was not much deceived
as to her own skill either
as an artist or a musician,
but she was not unwilling
to have others deceived, or
sorry to know her reputation
for accomplishment often
higher than it deserved.

OF EMMA WOODHOUSE, *EMMA*

'I am afraid, Mama, he has no real taste. Music seems scarcely to attract him, and though he admires Elinor's drawings very much, it is not the admiration of a person who can understand their worth.'

MARIANNE DASHWOOD ON EDWARD FERRARS, *SENSE AND SENSIBILITY*

———◆———

So far her improvement was sufficient – and in many other points she came on exceedingly well; for though she could not write sonnets, she brought herself to read them; and though there seemed no chance of her throwing a whole party into raptures by a prelude on the pianoforte, of her own composition, she could listen to other people's performance with very little fatigue.

OF CATHERINE MORLAND, *NORTHANGER ABBEY*

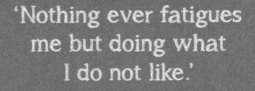

'Nothing ever fatigues
me but doing what
I do not like.'

MISS CRAWFORD, *MANSFIELD PARK*

There was a numerous family; but the only two grown up, excepting Charles, were Henrietta and Louisa, young ladies of nineteen and twenty, who had brought from school at Exeter all the usual stock of accomplishments, and were now like thousands of other young ladies, living to be fashionable, happy, and merry.

PERSUASION

———◆———

Their conversation turned upon those subjects, of which the free discussion has generally much to do in perfecting a sudden intimacy between two young ladies: such as dress, balls, flirtations, and quizzes.

NORTHANGER ABBEY

'There is a stubbornness about me that can never bear to be frightened at the will of others. My courage always rises at every attempt to intimidate me.'

ELIZABETH BENNET,
PRIDE AND PREJUDICE

From the time of their sitting down to table, it was a quick succession of busy nothings till the carriage came to the door.

MANSFIELD PARK

'There will be little rubs and disappointments everywhere, and we are all apt to expect too much; but then, if one scheme of happiness fails, human nature turns to another; if the first calculation is wrong, we make a second better: we find comfort somewhere.'

MRS GRANT, *MANSFIELD PARK*

———◆———

'If I had been treated in that forbidding sort of way, I should have gave it all up in despair. I could not have stood it.'

LUCY STEELE, *SENSE AND SENSIBILITY*

Had not Elinor, in the sad
countenance of her sister, seen
a check to all mirth, she could
have been entertained by
Mrs Jennings's endeavours to
cure a disappointment in love,
by a variety of sweetmeats
and olives, and a good fire.

SENSE AND SENSIBILITY

Personal size and mental sorrow have certainly no necessary proportions. A large bulky figure has as good a right to be in deep affliction, as the most graceful set of limbs in the world.

PERSUASION

———◆———

She could not help being vexed at the non-appearance of Mr Thorpe, for she not only longed to be dancing, but was likewise aware that, as the real dignity of her situation could not be known, she was sharing with the scores of other young ladies still sitting down all the discredit of wanting a partner.

OF CATHERINE MORLAND, *NORTHANGER ABBEY*

'Elinor has not my feelings, and therefore she may overlook it, and be happy with him. But it would have broke MY heart, had I loved him, to hear him read with so little sensibility.'

MARIANNE DASHWOOD,
SENSE AND SENSIBILITY

'The more I see of the world, the more am I dissatisfied with it; and every day confirms my belief of the inconsistency of all human characters, and of the little dependence that can be placed on the appearance of merit or sense.'

ELIZABETH BENNET, *PRIDE AND PREJUDICE*

'Let your conduct be the only harangue.'

EDMUND BERTRAM, *MANSFIELD PARK*

I do not want people to be very agreeable, as it saves me the trouble of liking them a great deal.

LETTER TO CASSANDRA

They gave themselves up wholly to their sorrow, seeking increase of wretchedness in every reflection that could afford it, and resolved against ever admitting consolation in future.

SENSE AND SENSIBILITY

He [Mr Darcy] then went away, and Miss
Bingley was left to all the satisfaction
of having forced him to say what
gave no one any pain but herself.

PRIDE AND PREJUDICE

———◆———

By requiring her longer continuance
in London it deprived her of the only
possible alleviation of her wretchedness,
the personal sympathy of her mother,
and doomed her to such society
and such scenes as must prevent her
ever knowing a moment's rest.

*OF MARIANNE DASHWOOD,
SENSE AND SENSIBILITY*

MISPLACED LOVE AND HEARTBREAK

'It is always incomprehensible to a man that a woman should ever refuse an offer of marriage. A man always imagines a woman to be ready for any body who asks her.'

EMMA WOODHOUSE, *EMMA*

———◆———

'I wonder who first discovered the efficacy of poetry in driving away love!'

ELIZABETH BENNET, *PRIDE AND PREJUDICE*

To you I shall say, as I have often said before, do not be in a hurry, the right man will come at last.

LETTER TO FANNY KNIGHT

'A fortnight's acquaintance is certainly very little. One cannot know what a man really is by the end of a fortnight. But if *we* do not venture somebody else will.'

MR BENNET, *PRIDE AND PREJUDICE*

———◆———

'I am glad I have done being in love with him.'

EMMA WOODHOUSE, *EMMA*

———◆———

To flatter and follow others, without being flattered and followed in turn, is but a state of half enjoyment.

PERSUASION

Friendship is certainly the finest balm for the pangs of disappointed love.

NORTHANGER ABBEY

'I cannot help feeling
for those that are
crossed in love.'

ELIZABETH WATSON, *THE WATSONS*

———◆———

'One is apt, I believe, to connect
assurance of manner with coquetry, and
to expect that an impudent address will
naturally attend and impudent mind.'

MRS VERNON, *LADY SUSAN*

———◆———

The visions of romance
were over.

OF CATHERINE MORLAND'S SHAME
AT BEING REBUKED BY HENRY TILNEY,
NORTHANGER ABBEY

'Dare not say that man forgets sooner than woman, that his love has an earlier death.'

CAPTAIN FREDERICK WENTWORTH,
PERSUASION

'I wish with all my soul his wife
may plague his heart out.'

MRS JENNINGS, *SENSE AND SENSIBILITY*

—◆—

If it were love, it might be simple, single,
successless love on her side alone.

EMMA

—◆—

'You have liked many a stupider person.'

ELIZABETH BENNET TO JANE BENNET REGARDING
MR BINGLEY, *PRIDE AND PREJUDICE*

'One does not love a place the less for having suffered in it, unless it has been all suffering, nothing but suffering.'

ANNE ELLIOT, *PERSUASION*

'I could easily forgive
his pride, if he had not mortified *mine*.'

ELIZABETH BENNET ON MR DARCY,
PRIDE AND PREJUDICE

———◆———

'In marrying a man indifferent
to me, all risk would have been
incurred, and all duty violated.'

ANNE ELLIOT, *PERSUASION*

———◆———

Perfect happiness, even in
memory, is not common.

EMMA

Charlotte laughed
heartily to think that
her husband could
not get rid of her.

SENSE AND SENSIBILITY

There was a great deal of friendly
and of compassionate attachment
on his side – but no love.

EMMA

———◆———

There could have been no two hearts so
open, no tastes so similar, no feelings
so in unison, no countenances so
beloved. Now they were as strangers;
nay, worse than strangers, for they
could never become acquainted.

PERSUASION

'You could not have made
the offer of your hand in any
possible way that would have
tempted me to accept it.'

ELIZABETH BENNET TO MR DARCY,
PRIDE AND PREJUDICE

THE HAPPY OCCASION

Nothing can be compared to the misery of being bound without Love, bound to one, and preferring another. That is a punishment which you do not deserve.

LETTER TO FANNY KNIGHT

———◆———

'A lady's imagination is very rapid; it jumps from admiration to love, from love to matrimony, in a moment.'

MR DARCY, *PRIDE AND PREJUDICE*

'To marry for money
I think the wickedest
thing in existence.'

CATHERINE MORLAND, *NORTHANGER ABBEY*

'Yes, quite a proposal of marriage; and a very good letter, at least she thought so.'

HARRIET SMITH'S THOUGHTS ON HER LETTER FROM MR MARTIN, *EMMA*

———◆———

Nobody minds having what is too good for them.

MANSFIELD PARK

———◆———

'It is very often nothing but our own vanity that deceives us. Women fancy admiration means more than it does.'

JANE BENNET, *PRIDE AND PREJUDICE*

'Oh! The best nature in the world – a wedding.'

EMMA WOODHOUSE EXPLAINING THE NATURE OF THE NEWS SHE HAS FOR MR KNIGHTLEY, *EMMA*

'I am happier even than Jane;
she only smiles, I laugh.'

ELIZABETH BENNET, *PRIDE AND PREJUDICE*

———◆———

Single women have a dreadful propensity
for being poor, which is one very strong
argument in favour of matrimony.

LETTER TO FANNY KNIGHT

———◆———

'She must be attached
to you, or she would not
have married you.'

ELINOR DASHWOOD TO MR WILLOUGHBY
ON HIS WIFE, *SENSE AND SENSIBILITY*

One may as well be
single if the wedding
is not to be in print.

LETTER TO ANNA LEFROY

And yet I do wish you to marry
very much, because I know you
will never be happy till you are.

LETTER TO FANNY KNIGHT

———◆———

I consider everybody as having
a right to marry once in their
lives for love, if they can.

LETTER TO CASSANDRA

'That is their duty,
each to endeavour to
give the other no cause
for wishing that he
or she had bestowed
themselves elsewhere.'

HENRY TILNEY, *NORTHANGER ABBEY*

'When two sympathetic hearts meet in the marriage state, matrimony may be called a happy life.'

MISS CRAWFORD, *MANSFIELD PARK*

—◆—

'Men of sense, whatever you may choose to say, do not want silly wives.'

MR KNIGHTLEY, *EMMA*

'Did you ever hear
the old song, "Going
to One Wedding
Brings on Another"?'

JOHN THORPE, *NORTHANGER ABBEY*

'It is well to have as many holds
upon happiness as possible.'

HENRY WOODHOUSE, *EMMA*

———◆———

'Speaking from my own observation,
[marriage] is a manoeuvring business.'

MISS CRAWFORD, *MANSFIELD PARK*

———◆———

Husbands and wives generally
understand when opposition will be vain.

PERSUASION

'I cannot think well of a man who sports with any woman's feelings; and there may often be a great deal more suffered than a stander-by can judge of.'

FANNY PRICE, *MANSFIELD PARK*

From politics, it was an
easy step to silence.

NORTHANGER ABBEY

———◆———

'Her character depends upon those
she is with; but in good hands she
will turn out a valuable woman.'

MR KNIGHTLEY, *EMMA*

———◆———

'I cannot speak well enough
to be unintelligible.'

CATHERINE MORLAND, *NORTHANGER ABBEY*

He smiled, looked
handsome, and said
many pretty things.

OF MR WICKHAM,
PRIDE AND PREJUDICE

'If I loved you less, I might be
able to talk about it more.'

MR KNIGHTLEY TO EMMA WOODHOUSE, *EMMA*

———◆———

I quit such odious subjects as
soon as I can, impatient to restore
everybody, not greatly in fault
themselves, to tolerable comfort.

MANSFIELD PARK

———◆———

'Laugh as much as you choose, but you
will not laugh me out of my opinion.'

JANE BENNET, *PRIDE AND PREJUDICE*

'I could not excuse a man's having more music than love – more ear than eye – a more acute sensibility to fine sounds than to my feelings.'

EMMA WOODHOUSE, *EMMA*

'Good-humoured, unaffected girls will not do for a man who has been used to sensible women. They are two distinct orders of being.'

EDMUND BERTRAM, *MANSFIELD PARK*

———◆———

'There is no charm equal to tenderness of heart.'

EMMA WOODHOUSE, *EMMA*

———◆———

'There is hardly any personal defect which an agreeable manner might not gradually reconcile one to.'

ANNE THORPE, *NORTHANGER ABBEY*

'My idea of good company... is the company of clever, well-informed people, who have a great deal of conversation.'

ANNE ELLIOT, *PERSUASION*

In seasons of cheerfulness, no temper could be more cheerful than hers, or possess, in a greater degree, that sanguine expectation of happiness which is happiness itself.

SENSE AND SENSIBILITY

———◆———

'Those who do not complain are never pitied.'

MRS BENNET, *PRIDE AND PREJUDICE*

———◆———

'Selfishness must always be forgiven you know, because there is no hope of a cure.'

MISS CRAWFORD, *MANSFIELD PARK*

'I always deserve
the best treatment,
because I never put
up with any other.'

EMMA WOODHOUSE, *EMMA*

Her own thoughts and reflections were habitually her best companions.

MANSFIELD PARK

———◆———

'My idea of him is, that he can adapt his conversation to the taste of every body, and has the power as well as the wish of being universally agreeable.'

EMMA WOODHOUSE ON
FRANK CHURCHILL, *EMMA*

———◆———

'A woman in love with one man cannot flirt with another.'

CATHERINE MORLAND, *NORTHANGER ABBEY*

'We neither of us perform to strangers.'

MR DARCY TO ELIZABETH BENNET, COMPARING HIS ART OF CONVERSATION WITH HER PIANO PLAYING, *PRIDE AND PREJUDICE*

Mrs Allen was... never satisfied with the day unless she spent the chief of it by the side of Mrs Thorpe, in what they called conversation, but in which there was scarcely ever any exchange of opinion, and not often any resemblance of subject, for Mrs Thorpe talked chiefly of her children, and Mrs Allen of her gowns.

NORTHANGER ABBEY

———◆———

Marianne was silent; it was impossible for her to say what she did not feel, however trivial the occasion; and upon Elinor therefore the whole task of telling lies when politeness required it, always fell.

SENSE AND SENSIBILITY

'You must learn some of my philosophy. Think only of the past as its remembrance gives you pleasure.'

ELIZABETH BENNET, *PRIDE AND PREJUDICE*

———◆———

There are people, who the more you do for them, the less they will do for themselves.

EMMA

———◆———

'How wonderful, how very wonderful the operations of time, and the changes of the human mind!'

FANNY PRICE, *MANSFIELD PARK*

'We do not look in great cities
for our best morality.'

EDWARD BERTRAM, *MANSFIELD PARK*

—◆—

'Do not give way to useless alarm;
though it is right to be prepared
for the worst, there is no occasion
to look on it as certain.'

MR GARDINER, *PRIDE AND PREJUDICE*

—◆—

'Business, you know, may bring money,
but friendship hardly ever does.'

JOHN KNIGHTLEY, *EMMA*

'But I hate to hear you talking
so like a fine gentleman,
and as if women were
all fine ladies, instead of
rational creatures. We
none of us expect to be in
smooth water all our days.'

SOPHIA CROFT, *PERSUASION*

Every moment had its
pleasures and its hope.

MANSFIELD PARK

'It is particularly incumbent on those
who never change their opinion, to be
secure of judging properly at first.'

ELIZABETH BENNET, *PRIDE AND PREJUDICE*

'Better be without sense, than
misapply it as you do.'

MR KNIGHTLEY, *EMMA*

'Indulge your imagination
in every possible flight.'

ELIZABETH BENNET,
PRIDE AND PREJUDICE

I am not at all in a
humour for writing; I must
write on till I am.

LETTER TO CASSANDRA

———◆———

'We are sent into this world to be
as extensively useful as possible,
and where some degree of strength
of mind is given, it is not a feeble
body which will excuse us.'

SANDITON

———◆———

'Vanity working on a
weak head, produces every
sort of mischief.'

MR KNIGHTLEY, *EMMA*

A lady, without a family, was the very best preserver of furniture in the world.

PERSUASION

'It is very difficult for the prosperous to be humble.'

FRANK CHURCHILL, *EMMA*

———◆———

'People themselves alter so much, that there is something new to be observed in them for ever.'

ELIZABETH BENNET, *PRIDE AND PREJUDICE*

———◆———

'Where there is a disposition to dislike, a motive will never be wanting.'

LADY SUSAN VERNON, *LADY SUSAN*

'They are much to be pitied who have not... been given a taste for nature in early life.'

EDMUND BERTRAM, *MANSFIELD PARK*

'Silly things do cease to be silly
if they are done by sensible
people in an impudent way.'

EMMA WOODHOUSE, *EMMA*

———◆———

'The interest of two thousand pounds
– how can a man live on it?'

JOHN DASHWOOD, *SENSE AND SENSIBILITY*

———◆———

'The person, be it gentleman or
lady, who has not pleasure in a good
novel must be intolerably stupid.'

HENRY TILNEY, *NORTHANGER ABBEY*

'Oh! do not attack
me with your watch.
A watch is always too fast
or too slow. I cannot be
dictated to by a watch.'

MISS CRAWFORD, *MANSFIELD PARK*

'Seven years would be insufficient to make some people acquainted with each other and seven days are more than enough for others.'

MARIANNE DASHWOOD, *SENSE AND SENSIBILITY*

———◆———

An artist cannot do anything slovenly.

LETTER TO CASSANDRA

———◆———

A mind lively and at ease, can do with seeing nothing, and can see nothing that does not answer.

EMMA

'Mr Wickham is blessed with such happy manners as may ensure his *making* friends – whether he may be equally capable of *retaining* them, is less certain.'

MR DARCY, *PRIDE AND PREJUDICE*

What dreadful hot weather we have! It keeps one in a continual state of inelegance.

LETTER TO CASSANDRA

———◆———

'One cannot have too large a party.'

MR WESTON, *EMMA*

———◆———

'Your countenance perfectly informs me that you were in company last night with the person whom you think the most agreeable in the world, the person who interests you at this present time, more than all the rest of the world put together.'

MRS SMITH, *PERSUASION*

'Nothing is more deceitful...
than the appearance of
humility. It is often only
carelessness of opinion, and
sometimes an indirect boast.'

MR DARCY, *PRIDE AND PREJUDICE*

'Sometimes one is guided by what they say of themselves, and very frequently by what other people say of them, without giving oneself time to deliberate and judge.'

ELINOR DASHWOOD, *SENSE AND SENSIBILITY*

———◆———

'I have a great opinion of her. Whenever I see her, she always curtseys and asks me how I do, in a very pretty manner.'

MR WOODHOUSE ON HANNAH THE HOUSEMAID, *EMMA*

———◆———

'We have all a better guide in ourselves, if we would attend to it, than any other person can be.'

FANNY PRICE, *MANSFIELD PARK*

'She is poor; she has sunk from the comforts she was born to; and, if she live to old age, must probably sink more. Her situation should secure your compassion.'

MR KNIGHTLEY ON MISS BATES, *EMMA*

'What have wealth or grandeur
to do with happiness?'
'Grandeur has but little,' said Elinor,
'but wealth has much to do with it.'

MARIANNE AND ELINOR DASHWOOD,
SENSE AND SENSIBILITY

—◆—

'I never in my life saw a man more intent
on being agreeable than Mr Elton. It is
downright labour to him where ladies
are concerned. With men he can be
rational and unaffected, but when he has
ladies to please, every feature works.'

JOHN KNIGHTLEY, *EMMA*

The melancholy part was
to see so many dozen
young women standing
by without partners, and
each of them with two
ugly naked shoulders.

LETTER TO CASSANDRA

HEALTH
AND
HAPPINESS

'The truth is, that in London it is always a sickly season. Nobody is healthy in London, nobody can be.'

MR WOODHOUSE, *EMMA*

———◆———

'Run mad as often as you choose, but do not faint.'

SOPHIA, *LOVE AND FREINDSHIP*

———◆———

'Know your own happiness. You want nothing but patience – or give it a more fascinating name, call it hope.'

MRS DASHWOOD, *SENSE AND SENSIBILITY*

'One fatal swoon
has cost me my life...
Beware of swoons,
Dear Laura.'

SOPHIA, *LOVE AND FREINDSHIP*

'Why not seize the pleasure at once?
How often is happiness destroyed by
preparation, foolish preparation!'

FRANK CHURCHILL, *EMMA*

—◆—

'You take delight in vexing me. You have
no compassion for my poor nerves.'
'You mistake me, my dear. I have a
high respect for your nerves. They
are my old friends. I have heard you
mention them with consideration
these last twenty years at least.'

MRS AND MR BENNET, *PRIDE AND PREJUDICE*

'To sit in the shade on a fine day, and look upon verdure, is the most perfect refreshment.'

FANNY PRICE, *MANSFIELD PARK*

Elizabeth continued her walk alone,
crossing field after field at a quick
pace, jumping over stiles and springing
over puddles with impatient activity,
and finding herself at last within view
of the house, with weary ankles,
dirty stockings, and a face glowing
with the warmth of exercise.

PRIDE AND PREJUDICE

———◆———

'A taste for flowers is always desirable
in your sex, as a means of getting
you out of doors, and tempting
you to more frequent exercise than
you would otherwise take.'

HENRY TILNEY, *NORTHANGER ABBEY*

'Miss Eliza Bennet, let me persuade
you to follow my example, and
take a turn about the room. I
assure you it is very refreshing after
sitting so long in one attitude.'

MISS BINGLEY, *PRIDE AND PREJUDICE*

———◆———

How quick come the reasons
for approving what we like.

PERSUASION

———◆———

It was absolutely necessary that
I should have the little fever and
indisposition, which I had; it has been
all the fashion this week in Lyme.

LETTER TO CASSANDRA

'There is nothing
like staying at home
for real comfort.'

MRS ELTON, *EMMA*

'I wish, as well as everybody else, to be perfectly happy; but, like everybody else, it must be in my own way.'

ELINOR DASHWOOD, *SENSE AND SENSIBILITY*

———◆———

I bought some Japan Ink likewise, and next week shall begin my operations on my hat, on which you know my principal hopes of happiness depend.

LETTER TO CASSANDRA

———◆———

A general spirit of ease and enjoyment seemed diffused, and they all stood about and talked and laughed, and every moment had its pleasure and its hope.

MANSFIELD PARK

WITTY
QUIPS

Mrs Portman is not much admired in Dorsetshire; the good-natured world, as usual, extolled her beauty so highly, that all the neighbourhood have had the pleasure of being disappointed.

LETTER TO CASSANDRA

——◆——

Mrs Allen was one of that numerous class of females, whose society can raise no other emotion than surprise at there being any men in the world who could like them well enough to marry them.

NORTHANGER ABBEY

'It is better to know as little as possible of the defects of the person with whom you are to pass your life.'

CHARLOTTE LUCAS,
PRIDE AND PREJUDICE

'If I could persuade myself that my manners were perfectly easy and graceful, I should not be shy.'

EDWARD FERRARS, *SENSE AND SENSIBILITY*

——◆——

'Surprises are foolish things. The pleasure is not enhanced, and the inconvenience is often considerable.'

MR KNIGHTLEY, *EMMA*

——◆——

'Every savage can dance.'

MR DARCY, *PRIDE AND PREJUDICE*

My hair was at least
tidy, which was
all my ambition.

LETTER TO CASSANDRA

'Stupid men are the only ones worth knowing, after all.'

ELIZABETH BENNET, *PRIDE AND PREJUDICE*

——◆——

It was a delightful visit; – perfect, in being much too short.

EMMA

——◆——

'People always live for ever when there is an annuity to be paid them.'

FANNY DASHWOOD, *SENSE AND SENSIBILITY*

'Brandon is just the kind of man,' said Willoughby one day, when they were talking of him together, 'whom every body speaks well of, and nobody cares about; whom all are delighted to see, and nobody remembers to talk to.'

SENSE AND SENSIBILITY

Another stupid party last night; perhaps if larger they might be less intolerable, but here there were only just enough to make one card-table, with six people to look on and talk nonsense to each other.

LETTER TO CASSANDRA

———◆———

'One half of the world cannot understand the pleasures of the other.'

EMMA WOODHOUSE, *EMMA*

———◆———

Lady Middleton was more agreeable than her mother only in being more silent.

SENSE AND SENSIBILITY

The Miss Maitlands are both prettyish... with brown skins, large dark eyes, and a good deal of nose. – The General has got the gout, and Mrs Maitland the jaundice. – Miss Debary, Susan and Sally... made their appearance, and I was as civil to them as their bad breath would allow me.

LETTER TO CASSANDRA

'You must try not to mind growing
up into a pretty woman.'

EDMUND BERTRAM, *MANSFIELD PARK*

———◆——

I will not say that your mulberry-trees are
dead, but I am afraid they are not alive.

LETTER TO CASSANDRA

———◆——

Pictures of perfection,
as you know, make me sick and wicked.

LETTER TO FANNY KNIGHT

'A clergyman has nothing to do but be slovenly and selfish – read the newspaper, watch the weather, and quarrel with his wife. His curate does all the work, and the business of his own life is to dine.'

MISS CRAWFORD, *MANSFIELD PARK*

No man is offended by another man's admiration for the woman he loves; it is the woman only who can make it a torment.

NORTHANGER ABBEY

——◆——

Wisdom is better than wit, and in the long run will certainly have the laugh on her side.

LETTER TO FANNY KNIGHT

——◆——

'For what do we live, but to make sport for our neighbours, and laugh at them in our turn?'

MR BENNET, PRIDE AND PREJUDICE